STUDENT GUIDE

Abingdon Press
Nashville

AFFIRM STUDENT GUIDE

Writer: Audrey Wilder
Editor: Sara Galyon

Websites are constantly changing. Although the websites recommended in this resource were checked at the time this unit was developed, we recommend that you double-check all sites to verify that they are still live and that they are still suitable for students before doing an activity.

ISBN: 9781501867729

PACP10537567-01

18 19 20 21 22 23 24 25 26 27 — 10 9 8 7 6 5 4 3 2 1

MANUFACTURED IN THE UNITED STATES OF AMERICA

Contents

Welcome 5

Lesson 1: The Faith Journey 6

Lesson 2: The Faith Given to You 20

Lesson 3: Life in Christ 36

Lesson 4: Know What You Believe 50

Lesson 5: Know Why You Believe 66

Lesson 6: Hearing God Speak 80

Welcome to your AFFIRM journal! This is the place where you will start to think about the week's topic and do some walking of your journey with God by yourself. We call this Solo Searching. You'll also use this journal as you are walking with your peers through this study. However, know that this is your personal journal, and you will never be forced to share your reflections or ideas with anyone beyond God.

Lesson 1: The Faith Journey

SUMMARY

We will start by reflecting on *transformation*. Since the point of participating in any kind of small-group study is to somehow be changed by the experience, it seems a good enough place to start. This week's devotions will help you figure out what transformation means to you and how it could be important in your walk with God.

OVERVIEW

1) **Connect** through a choice of activities that challenge students to explore the practical aspects of transformation.

2) **Explore** how Paul encourages the early Christian church to be agents of transformation.

3) **Reflect** on what transformation means personally.

4) **Create** encouragement for statements to help others in their journey of transformation.

5) **Next,** practice becoming a person who lives a transformed life every day

ANCHOR POINT

Philippians 1:6 — I'm sure about this: the one who started a good work in you will stay with you to complete the job by the day of Christ Jesus.

Affirm

SOLO SEARCHING

Stop 1—Defining Transformation

Step 1—Get on Instagram and search *#transformation*. Based on what you see, define transformation according to Instagram.

Step 2—Find a dictionary (online or on a bookshelf) and write down one of the definitions of transformation you find.

Step 3—Read Acts 9:1-22 and write down your own definition of transformation based on this Scripture passage.

Step 4—Reflect and Respond

Based on what you have seen and read, what is required for a transformation to take place?

When is transformation a solo act?

When is transformation a group project?

Who would you want in your transformation group and why?

Affirm
Stop 2—Painful Transformation

Step 1—Find a picture of yourself around kindergarten (five years old), fifth grade (ten years old), and now. Place the pictures side by side and write down a few things that changed in your physical appearance over the years.

Step 2—Read Genesis 32:22-31 below.

1) The first time you read it, highlight any words or phrases that lead you to believe Jacob was struggling or in pain.

2) Read the passage a second time, underlining words or phrases that indicate Jacob was transforming.

3) Read the passage a third time, circling any words or phrases that remind you of a time when you were struggling, in pain, or going through some sort of transformation.

Jacob got up during the night, took his two wives, his two women servants, and his eleven sons, and crossed the Jabbok River's shallow water. He took them and everything that belonged to him, and he helped them cross the river. But Jacob stayed apart by himself, and a man wrestled with him until dawn broke. When the man saw that he couldn't defeat Jacob, he grabbed Jacob's thigh and tore a muscle in Jacob's thigh as he wrestled with him. The man said, "Let me go because the dawn is breaking."

But Jacob said, "I won't let you go until you bless me."

He said to Jacob, "What's your name?" and he said, "Jacob." Then he said, "Your name won't be Jacob any longer, but Israel, because you struggled with God and with men and won."

Jacob also asked and said, "Tell me your name."

But he said, "Why do you ask for my name?" and he blessed Jacob there. Jacob named the place Peniel, "because I've seen God face-to-face, and my life has been saved." The sun rose as Jacob passed Penuel, limping because of his thigh.

Step 3—Reflect and Respond

Jacob didn't walk away from his struggle with God without any pain. Jacob limped away with his life and a new name. Transformation is not always painful, but there is opportunity for transformation in every painful experience of our lives. Jacob could have given up when he was injured, but instead he demanded God transform him.

Think about the most difficult change you have faced in your life. Write down three painful consequences of that change and three joyful results of that change.

Painful —   Joyful —

1)   1)

2)   2)

3)   3)

How is God with you in both pain and joy?

The next time you have a painful experience, what will you do to remind yourself of God's presence? How will you look for ways to experience transformation?

Optional additional Scripture reading: Romans 5:1-5.

Affirm

TEAM TRAVELING

CONNECT

Things That Transform

With your partner, talk for about a minute-and-a-half about what is required for your object to transform.

Group Discussion Questions

- What do you think transformation means?

- What is required for something to transform into something else?

- How long does transformation take?

Who's Who?

How many baby pictures did you guess correctly?

Group Discussion Questions

- What kinds of physical changes are most common in growing from a baby to a teenager?

- What traits typically stay with us as we grow older?

- How do our relationships change as we grow older?

- What feelings are associated with changing into a different person?

EXPLORE

As you read the following passage, underline words or phrases that indicate forward progression or a change for an individual.

Philippians 1:3-11: I thank my God every time I mention you in my prayers. I'm thankful for all of you every time I pray, and it's always a prayer full of joy. I'm glad because of the way you have been my partners in the ministry of the gospel from the time you first believed it until now. I'm sure about this: the one who started a good work in you will stay with you to complete the job by the day of Christ Jesus. I have good reason to think this way about all of you because I keep you in my heart. You are all my partners in God's grace, both during my time in prison and in the defense and support of the gospel. God is my witness that I feel affection for all of you with the compassion of Christ Jesus.

This is my prayer: that your love might become even more and more rich with knowledge and all kinds of insight. I pray this so that you will be able to decide what really matters and so you will be sincere and blameless on the day of Christ. I pray that you will then be filled with the fruit of righteousness, which comes from Jesus Christ, in order to give glory and praise to God.

Questions for Consideration

- When you receive a message of encouragement, how does it make you feel? Why?

- Why would it be important for Paul to start a letter with such encouragement?

- If your pastor was to write a letter like this to you, how would that make you feel?

Notes about Paul's transformation story:

- If you have ever had someone say to you, "I am praying for you," what kind of difference did that make in your life?

- What is the difference between Paul saying, "I am praying that you will do these things," and "I think you really need to be doing better at these things"?

- What do you think the role of prayer is in a person becoming more like Christ?

- How does the support of fellow believers impact the development of a person's relationship with Christ?

- How could being in relationship with people who have been transformed by God help shape your own transformation?

R E F L E C T

Philippians 1:6: I'm sure about this: the one who started a good work in you will stay with you to complete the job by the day of Christ Jesus.

- Can you think of ways God has worked in other people to impact your life? List them here:

- What "good work" did God start because of you?

- What work do you think God has for you to do in the next few months?

- Is there something you've thought about doing for God, but never have actually done? What has stopped you from getting started? What do you need to take the first step?

CREATE

In your groups of three, come up with at least three encouraging statements you could share with other members of the group to help them when transformation gets hard or when they feel stuck.

Encouraging Statement 1

Encouraging Statement 2

Encouraging Statement 3

Discussion Questions

- Why might it be dangerous to compare your transformation, or your walk with Christ, to someone else's?

- Do you think you have a responsibility to become involved with someone else's personal relationship with God? If yes, how do you do that? If no, why not?

- How can God use the painful experiences we go through to make us more like Christ?

- How would your life be different if, each morning when you woke up, you made a promise to yourself and God that "Today, I'm going to do one thing that makes me more like Christ"?

N E X T

I pray this so that you will be able to decide what really matters and so you will be sincere and blameless on the day of Christ. I pray that you will then be filled with the fruit of righteousness, which comes from Jesus Christ, in order to give glory and praise to God (Philippians 1:10-11).

This week, every morning when you're brushing your teeth, think of one thing you will do that will reflect Christ's image. Write it down here:

Day 1—

Day 2—

Day 3—

Day 4—

Day 5—

Day 6—

Using one of the encouragement statements or pictures from today's session, send someone not in this study a Snapchat, text, email, or letter to encourage them in their faith journey.

Lesson 2: The Faith Given to You

SUMMARY

The question you will be considering this week is "Where does your faith come from?" We do not come to faith on our own; we have others who teach us about God and show us what it means to live out our faith. Ultimately, however, having faith in God is a personal commitment that requires every individual to make decisions about what they will believe and how they will live out that belief.

OVERVIEW

1) **Connect** though activities that get students thinking about what Christians do.

2) **Explore** the use of metaphor as a way to make talking about faith more approachable.

3) **Reflect** individually on core beliefs and the role tradition plays in faith development.

4) **Create** a blueprint of your faith, considering who helped build the different parts of your faith.

5) **Next,** become the builder and determine who God is calling you to help build up.

ANCHOR POINT

1 Corinthians 3:5-6—After all, what is Apollos? What is Paul? They are servants who helped you to believe. Each one had a role given to them by the Lord: I planted, Apollos watered, but God made it grow.

Affirm
SOLO SEARCHING

Prayer: Jesus, help me see you along this journey. Amen.

Stop 1—Faith from the Wilderness

Step 1—Write below a list of things you do after school on the busiest day of your week. Start the list with the first thing you do after classes, and end your list with the last thing you do before you go to bed.

Step 2—Review your list and circle anything on the list that makes you complain or causes you frustration.

Step 3—Read the selections for Exodus 16 on the following page. If you have time, it might help to read all of Exodus 16.

The Israelites had been freed from slavery in Egypt by God through Moses and Aaron. This huge community of people were two-and-a-half months into their freedom when they started to complain, a lot!

Exodus 16:2-5 — The whole Israelite community complained against Moses and Aaron in the desert. The Israelites said to them, "Oh, how we wish that the Lord had just put us to death while we were still in the land of Egypt. There we could sit by the pots cooking meat and eat our fill of bread. Instead, you've brought us out into this desert to starve this whole assembly to death."

Then the Lord said to Moses, "I'm going to make bread rain down from the sky for you. The people will go out each day and gather just enough for that day. In this way, I'll test them to see whether or not they follow my instruction. On the sixth day, when they measure out what they have collected, it will be twice as much as they collected on other days."

Exodus 16:13-15 — In the evening a flock of quail flew down and covered the camp. And in the morning there was a layer of dew all around the camp. When the layer of dew lifted, there on the desert surface were thin flakes, as thin as frost on the ground. When the Israelites saw it, they said to each other, "What is it?" They didn't know what it was.

Moses said to them, "This is the bread that the Lord has given you to eat."

Exodus 16:31-32 — The Israelite people called it manna. It was like coriander seed, white, and tasted like honey wafers. Moses said, "This is what the Lord has commanded: 'Let an omer of it be kept safe for future generations so that they can see the food that I used to feed you in the desert when I brought you out of the land of Egypt.'"

Even though the people were complaining and didn't do what God asked them to do, God still gave them quail and manna.

Step 4—Review your after-school schedule again. Underline the things you do that bring you joy or comfort.

Step 5—Reflect and Respond

Compare the things you circled and those you underlined.

How long do you spend on the things that cause complaint, and how long on the things that bring you joy?

If you think about the activities that bring you joy as your "manna moments," then how do they help you through the other parts of your day?

How do you create more "manna moments"? How could God turn your complaining activities into "manna moments"?

Why do "manna moments" help us to have faith in God?

Prayer: Jesus, bring me joy along this journey. Amen.

Stop 2—Hope for the Unbelievable

Prayer: Jesus, give me hope along this journey. Amen.

Step 1—Read the following selections from Hebrews 11.

By faith we understand that the universe has been created by a word from God so that the visible came into existence from the invisible (11:3).

By faith Noah responded with godly fear when he was warned about events he hadn't seen yet. He built an ark to deliver his household. With his faith, he criticized the world and became an heir of the righteousness that comes from faith (11:7).

By faith Abraham obeyed when he was called to go out to a place that he was going to receive as an inheritance. He went out without knowing where he was going (11:8).

By faith even Sarah received the ability to have a child, though she herself was barren and past the age for having children, because she believed that the one who promised was faithful (11:11).

By faith Moses was hidden by his parents for three months when he was born, because they saw that the child was beautiful and they weren't afraid of the king's orders (11:23).

By faith Jericho's walls fell after the people marched around them for seven days (11:30).

Step 2—Circle the person you think had the most faith.

What was she or he hoping for?

What change did she or he believe was coming, but hadn't seen yet?

Step 3—*Hebrews 11:1-2 says: Faith is the reality of what we hope for, the proof of what we don't see. The elders in the past were approved because they showed faith.*

Draw a picture below of something you hope for the world.

Draw a picture below of something you believe in, but you cannot see.

Step 4—Reflect and Respond

How do you think hope and faith are connected?

Where does your faith come from? What things have happened in your life to give you faith in God?

How would you respond to someone asking you to explain why you believed in something you cannot see?

Prayer: Jesus, help me see along this journey. Amen.

TRAVELING TOGETHER

CONNECT

Never Have I Ever and What Is Necessary?

Write down a few of the "Christians Do" statements you think are problematic.

Group Discussion Questions

- Looking at these "Christians Do" statements, which ones seem to cause Christians to judge one another the most? Why do you think we do that?

- How do you tell the difference between how God wants you to grow your faith and how others think you should grow your faith?

- Imagine you are new to the Christian faith. What would you feel looking at this deck of cards?

- How do we help non-Christians or new Christians see the Christian faith as more than a "to-do list"?

EXPLORE

Reader 1 — 1 Corinthians 3:4-8

When someone says, "I belong to Paul," and someone else says, "I belong to Apollos," aren't you acting like people without the Spirit? After all, what is Apollos? What is Paul? They are servants who helped you to believe. Each one had a role given to them by the Lord: I planted, Apollos watered, but God made it grow. Because of this, neither the one who plants nor the one who waters is anything, but the only one who is anything is God who makes it grow. The one who plants and the one who waters work together, but each one will receive their own reward for their own labor.

Reader 2 — 1 Corinthians 3:9-11

We are God's coworkers, and you are God's field, God's building. I laid a foundation like a wise master builder according to God's grace that was given to me, but someone else is building on top of it. Each person needs to pay attention to the way they build on it. No one can lay any other foundation besides the one that is already laid, which is Jesus Christ.

Make Your Own Metaphor

Forming your own faith is like . . .

In your group, again read 1 Corinthians 3:4-11. Using what Paul is saying about forming your own faith and other metaphors in Scripture, create your own modern-day metaphor for how a person forms their own faith.

Your group may also choose to draw a simile (again, still a metaphor; just a specific kind), instead of writing a metaphor. You can illustrate what it is like for a person to form their own faith.

Whether writing a metaphor or drawing a simile, please be sure to consider including:

- Who is involved and how (example: baker mixing ingredients)

- How core beliefs are learned (how ingredients are added — poured, cracked, sifted, and so forth)

- What happens when there are setbacks/things go wrong (don't have enough vanilla)

- Role God plays in faith (oven fuses all ingredients together)

REFLECT

No one can lay any other foundation besides the one that is already laid, which is Jesus Christ (1 Corinthians 3:11).

• List three core beliefs you have about Jesus:

1 —

2 —

3 —

• What do you believe to be true about Jesus?

• What is something you've been taught that you are not sure you believe?

• What is one practice of the church you would like to change? Why and how?

CREATE

Beside each portion of the house, write the name of someone who has been a construction worker for building your faith. If you can remember specific things they taught you or ways they taught you, note those as well.

Foundation: Who has been most influential in teaching you who Jesus is?

Floor joists: Who has been most influential in teaching you about the Bible?

Window frame: Who has taught you how to look at others through the eyes of Jesus?

Studs: Who helps you understand the role God plays in your everyday life?

Roof: Who has shown you God's love and protection?

Front door: Who has taught you how to welcome others into the family of God?

Garage: Who has taught you how to go out and share your faith with others?

Who Are You Building Up?

Think about parts of your faith in which you are confident.
Do you sing well? Are you a good public speaker? Do you
have a good understanding of what Jesus means when he uses
metaphor or parables? Can you write great prayers?

In the circle on the following page, write one way you can help
someone grow their faith. (How can you be a construction
worker in their faith?)

At the end of the arrows, write the names of three people you
think God is calling you to help.

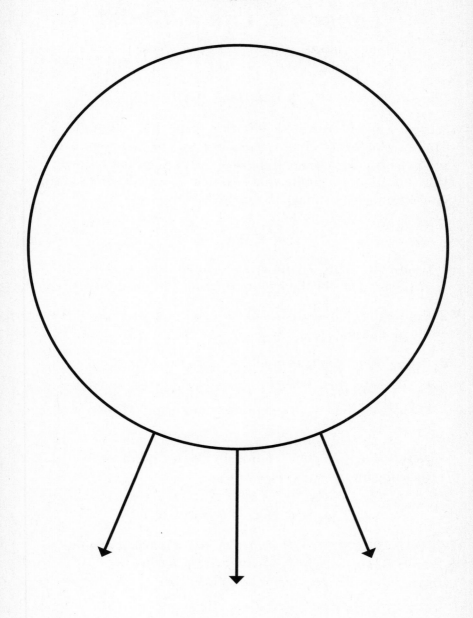

Lesson 3: Life in Christ

SUMMARY

A life in Christ is distinctly different than a life without Christ. There are many different ways to live out our faith, but living in Christ is not the same thing as living out our faith. Living in Christ is about reflecting God to others in what we do and say, and the choices we make in the way we live.

OVERVIEW

1) **Connect** through activities to get students focused on character traits or the fruit of the Spirit in the group.

2) **Explore** the characteristics of God and how we embody the divine image.

3) **Reflect** on how anti-fruit of the Spirit can impact our relationship with God.

4) **Create** a church event celebrating and using every fruit of the Spirit.

5) **Next,** strengthen your relationship with God through focusing on the fruit of the Spirit.

ANCHOR POINT

Galatians 5:22-23 — But the fruit of the Spirit is love, joy, peace, patience, kindness, goodness, faithfulness, gentleness, and self-control. There is no law against things like this.

S O L O   S E A R C H I N G

Stop 1: Looking in the Mirror

Prayer: God, show me yourself along this journey. Amen.

Step 1—Read Ephesians 5:1-2 below:

Therefore, imitate God like dearly loved children. Live your life with love, following the example of Christ, who loved us and gave himself for us. He was a sacrificial offering that smelled sweet to God.

Step 2—Make a list of things people imitate.

Step 3—John Wesley, the founder of Methodism, believed there were practices, or disciplines, that Christ-followers could work on that would help them become more like Christ. There are two categories of the disciplines, known as the means of grace. There are the works of piety and the works of mercy.

When you practice the means of grace, three things happen:

A. You begin to act and sound like Christ. (You are transformed.)

B. Your relationship with God grows stronger. (Your relationship is transformed.)

C. The people surrounding you begin to see God through you. (The world is transformed.)

Step 4—Beside each work of piety or mercy, write or comment or draw a sketch of when or how Jesus set the example (for example: Study Scripture—Jesus in the temple three days).

Works of Piety
Read Scripture
Bible Study
Pray
Fast
Worship

Live Healthy
Share Your Faith
Communion
Christian Accountability

Works of Mercy

Doing Good Works
Visit the Sick
Visit Prisoners
Feed the Hungry
Give Generously
Seek Justice
End Oppression
End Discrimination
Address the Needs of the Poor

Step 5—Reflect and Respond

Who do you want to be when you grow up?

Why should you want to be like Christ?

How can the means of grace help focus your life in Christ?

Prayer: God, make me like you along this journey. Amen.

Stop 2—Go Do It

Prayer: God, keep me safe along this journey. Amen.

Step 1—Read James 1:22-25.

You must be doers of the word and not only hearers who mislead themselves. Those who hear but don't do the word are like those who look at their faces in a mirror. They look at themselves, walk away, and immediately forget what they were like. But there are those who study the perfect law, the law of freedom, and continue to do it. They don't listen and then forget, but they put it into practice in their lives. They will be blessed in whatever they do.

Step 2— Review the **Works of Mercy** from "Stop 1." Choose one that you can do before the next group study. Write it down here and then go do it! Move on to Step 3 after you've done it.

Step 3—Reflect and Respond

Where did you see God in the person(s) you served?

How did you reflect God as you served?

How would serving like this every week change your life in Christ?

Prayer: God, show me where to serve along this journey. Amen.

TRAVELING TOGETHER

CONNECT

Person Pictionary

Following the game:

• Compare how the illustrators chose to depict the person.

• Did getting two different types of clues impact the depiction? If so, how?

• What was the final part of the drawing that made you realize who they were depicting?

Red Light, Yellow Light, Green Light

Red — Not so good at it

Yellow — Moderately good at it

Green — Got it down

Fruit of the Spirit

Love

Joy

Peace

Patience

Kindness

Goodness

Faithfulness

Gentleness

Self-control

- How do you think the presence of the fruit of the Spirit might impact our outreach and the perceptions of non-Christians about our church?

EXPLORE

Find and read the Scripture passages assigned to your group. List the character traits of your assigned member of the Trinity on a large piece of paper given to you by your leaders. There is also room beside each passage for you to take your own notes as you read.

God Squad

2 Peter 3:5-9

Psalm 116:5-9

Jeremiah 10:12-13

Numbers 14:18-23

John 1:1-5

Isaiah 40:28-31

Luke 1:26-37

1 John 4:7-16

Jesus Squad

John 1:1-5

John 1:10-18, 29-34

1 John 4:7-16

Matthew 9:2-8

Mark 10:39-45

John 14:1-13

Luke 1:26-37

Holy Spirit Squad

John 1:29-34

Luke 1:26-37

1 John 4:7-16

John 14:15-17, 25-26

John 16:7-15

1 Corinthians 12:1-11

Acts 2:1-4, 16-18, 32-33

Acts 19:1-7

1 Corinthians 2:9-15

Affirm

Genesis 1:26-27: Then God said, "Let us make humanity in our image to resemble us so that they may take charge of the fish of the sea, the birds in the sky, the livestock, all the earth, and all the crawling things on earth."

God created humanity in God's own image,

> *in the divine image God created them,*

>> *male and female God created them.*

Galatians 5:22-23: But the fruit of the Spirit is love, joy, peace, patience, kindness, goodness, faithfulness, gentleness, and self-control. There is no law against things like this.

Questions for Consideration

- What connections do you see between character traits of God and the fruit of the Spirit?

- How can the fruit of the Spirit help us better understand God and improve our relationship with God?

- If the fruit of the Spirit isn't something we do but something God does in us, then how do we get God to do it?

- How does the fruit of the Spirit allow humanity to reflect the divine image?

- What happens when we begin to resemble God?

REFLECT

Read Galatians 5:25-26:

If we live by the Spirit, let's follow the Spirit. Let's not become arrogant, make each other angry, or be jealous of each other.

Beside each component of the fruit of the Spirit below, write what you believe would be an antonym (or opposite) of that word.

For example: Next to *Peace,* you may write *Anxiety.*

Love

Joy

Peace

Patience

Kindness

Goodness

Faithfulness

Gentleness

Self-control

- Which of these anti-fruit separates you from God the most?

- How is your anti-fruit impacting your resemblance of God?

- How can arrogance, anger, or jealousy turn the fruit of the Spirit into an anti-fruit?

Fruit-of-the-Spirit Church Event

As a group, you are going to plan a mock church event. This mock event should allow all participants to experience all the components of the fruit of the Spirit.

- Who's invited?

- What will the invited do?

- What will the people hosting do? What are their responsibilities?

- What conflicts may arise, and how will they be handled?

- How will each of the components of the fruit of the Spirit be exhibited?

Love

Joy

Peace

Patience

Kindness

Goodness

Faithfulness

Gentleness

Self-control

Think of someone whom you believe shows the fruit of the Spirit often. Send them a text/note thanking them for their example, ask them to pray for you so you can do better showing others the fruit of the Spirit.

You can draft your text or your note in the space below.

Lesson 4: Know What You Believe

S U M M A R Y

It is highly probable that you know someone in your circle of friends, relatives, or neighbors who does not believe that God matters. Part of growing in faith is being able to explain to others why God matters and what difference God makes. There are many reasons why God matters, and it takes a lifetime to fully explore all of them. This week you will focus on why God's love matters most for others and for you.

O V E R V I E W

1) **Connect** through a choice of activities that challenges the students to think about partnership and love.

2) **Explore** the impact God's sacrificial love has on the world, our communities, and individuals.

3) **Reflect** on what difference you have seen God make.

4) **Create** annotated belief statements for a limited character world.

5) **Next,** discover ways God shows us love each day.

A N C H O R   P O I N T

Ephesians 2:8-9 — You are saved by God's grace because of your faith. This salvation is God's gift. It's not something you possessed. It's not something you did that you can be proud of.

SOLO SEARCHING

Stop 1: Who do you say that I am?

Prayer: Christ, set me free from sin along this journey. Amen.

Step 1—Read Matthew 16:13-20 below. As you read, underline or highlight any words or phrases that stick out to you.

Now when Jesus came to the area of Caesarea Philippi, he asked his disciples, "Who do people say the Human One is?"

They replied, "Some say John the Baptist, others Elijah, and still others Jeremiah or one of the other prophets."

He said, "And what about you? Who do you say that I am?"

Simon Peter said, "You are the Christ, the Son of the living God."

Then Jesus replied, "Happy are you, Simon son of Jonah, because no human has shown this to you. Rather my Father who is in heaven has shown you. I tell you that you are Peter. And I'll build my church on this rock. The gates of the underworld won't be able to stand against it. I'll give you the keys of the kingdom of heaven. Anything you fasten on earth will be fastened in heaven. Anything you loosen on earth will be loosened in heaven." Then he ordered the disciples not to tell anybody that he was the Christ.

Step 2—Listen

Go to YouTube and search, "Who You Say I Am," by Hillsong. Listen to the song. As you listen, write down any words or phrases that stick out to you.

Step 3—Compare

Look at what you highlighted in the Scripture passage from Matthew and the lyrics.

Based on what stood out to you in both, what do you think God is saying to you?

What do you think God wants you to know about your relationship?

Step 4—Reflect and Respond

Why do you think people were confused about who Jesus was?

What is still confusing to you about who Jesus is?

What does Jesus' sacrifice for you tell you about God?

What does Jesus' sacrifice for you tell you about yourself?

Prayer: Christ, fasten me to you along this journey. Amen.

Stop 2: Who are you looking for?

Prayer: Christ, reveal yourself to me along this journey. Amen.

Step 1—Read John 20:11-18:

Mary stood outside near the tomb, crying. As she cried, she bent down to look into the tomb. She saw two angels dressed in white, seated where the body of Jesus had been, one at the head and one at the foot. The angels asked her, "Woman, why are you crying?"

She replied, "They have taken away my Lord, and I don't know where they've put him." As soon as she had said this, she turned around and saw Jesus standing there, but she didn't know it was Jesus.

Jesus said to her, "Woman, why are you crying? Who are you looking for?"

Thinking he was the gardener, she replied, "Sir, if you have carried him away, tell me where you have put him and I will get him."

Jesus said to her, "Mary." She turned and said to him in Aramaic, "Rabbouni" (which means Teacher).

Jesus said to her, "Don't hold on to me, for I haven't yet gone up to my Father. Go to my brothers and sisters and tell them, 'I'm going up to my Father and your Father, to my God and your God.'"

Mary Magdalene left and announced to the disciples, "I've seen the Lord." Then she told them what he said to her.

Step 2—Search for the following pieces of art of John 20:

- *The Appearance to Mary Magdalene (drawing)*, Ferdinand Bol

- *Noli Me Tangere (Touch Me Not)*, James Tissot

- *The Empty Tomb*, He Qi

What is similar in the art pieces? What is different?

Which one do you think brings the story to life the most? Why?

Step 3—Make your own.

Draw what you imagine the scene to look like. Use these questions to help you focus:

- What for you is the most important part of this story?

- Who do you connect with in this story?

- What does this story make you feel?

Affirm

Step 4—Reflect and Respond

How can art help us to understand or connect to Scripture better?

Why do you think two of the three pieces of artwork have Mary Magdalene in the center?

What can you learn from Mary Magdalene in this passage?

Prayer: Christ, dry my tears along this journey. Amen.

TRAVELING TOGETHER

CONNECT

Somebody with You

Discussion Questions

- How was the game different for the person who did it on their own versus the person who had a partner?

- Who was more efficient in the problem-solving? Why?

- Did it seem fair that one person had support and the other did not? Why was it fair or not fair?

- How does having a partner make problems more manageable?

- How does knowing you have support impact the belief that you will succeed?

Love Lyrics

Write down as many lyrics about love as you can think of:

Discussion Questions

- What do lyrics about love have in common?

- How does music help us talk about love?

- How can music help to explain God's love to people who might not get it?

EXPLORE

Team Past—**Ephesians 2:4-9**

However, God is rich in mercy. He brought us to life with Christ while we were dead as a result of those things that we did wrong. He did this because of the great love that he has for us. You are saved by God's grace! And God raised us up and seated us in the heavens with Christ Jesus. God did this to show future generations the greatness of his grace by the goodness that God has shown us in Christ Jesus.

You are saved by God's grace because of your faith. This salvation is God's gift. It's not something you possessed. It's not something you did that you can be proud of.

Answer the following questions based on your reading.

• How did God's actions impact the world?

• How did God's actions impact humanity?

• How will God's actions impact your life?

Team Future — **Revelation 21:1-5**

Then I saw a new heaven and a new earth, for the former heaven and the former earth had passed away, and the sea was no more. I saw the holy city, New Jerusalem, coming down out of heaven from God, made ready as a bride beautifully dressed for her husband. I heard a loud voice from the throne say, "Look! God's dwelling is here with humankind. He will dwell with them, and they will be his peoples. God himself will be with them as their God. He will wipe away every tear from their eyes. Death will be no more. There will be no mourning, crying, or pain anymore, for the former things have passed away." Then the one seated on the throne said, "Look! I'm making all things new."

Answer the following questions based on your reading:

- How did God's actions impact the world?

- How did God's actions impact humanity?

- How will God's actions impact your life?

[God] brought us to life with Christ while we were dead as a result of those things that we did wrong. He did this because of the great love that he has for us (Ephesians 2:4-5).

- What difference has God made in your life?

- How has God impacted the life of someone you know?

- Write about a time when you felt God didn't matter.

- Sketch below a moment in your life when you knew God was close to you.

CREATE

Choose one of these three ways to say what you believe about either God, faith, or being a Christian.

1) Tweet It—Use only 280 characters, no emojis, to explain who God is to you.

2) Six-word memoir—Use only six words to tell your faith story (example: Jesus died so I can live).

3) 25 words or fewer—Use no more than 25 words to explain what it means to be a Christian.

- Group statement:

Today—In the heart shape below, write down one act of love you have seen during this session together.

This week, every evening when you're brushing your teeth, think of one act of love you experienced today. Write it down here and at the end of the week, review all the ways God has loved you this week.

Day 1—

Day 2—

Day 3—

Day 4—

Day 5—

Day 6—

PRAYER

Our father, who art in heaven,

hallowed be thy name.

Thy kingdom come,

thy will be done on earth as it is in heaven.

Give us this day our daily bread.

And forgive us our trespasses,

as we forgive those who trespass against us.

And lead us not into temptation,

but deliver us from evil.

For thine is the kingdom, and the power, and the glory,

forever. Amen.

Lesson 5: Know Why You Believe

SUMMARY

After having spent some time exploring the foundation of your belief in God's love, it's time to think about why you believe in God. We often don't take time to think about why we believe or ask God to help us understand why we believe. This week's devotions will be opportunities to pray your way into deeper belief.

OVERVIEW

1) **Connect** through a choice of activities that will challenge the students to think about how they share what they believe to be true about God.

2) **Explore** what Scripture tells us about God's expectations for followers of Christ.

3) **Reflect** on barriers that keep us from sharing God's love.

4) **Create** a plan for addressing common concerns for nonbelievers.

5) **Next,** see where other churches or denomination stand.

ANCHOR POINT

Matthew 25:21—His master replied, "Excellent! You are a good and faithful servant! You've been faithful over a little. I'll put you in charge of much. Come, celebrate with me."

SOLO SEARCHING

Stop 1—Help My Unbelief

Prayer: Holy Spirit, save me from pain along this journey. Amen.

Step 1—Read Mark 9:20-27.

They brought him. When the spirit saw Jesus, it immediately threw the boy into a fit. He fell on the ground and rolled around, foaming at the mouth. Jesus asked his father, "How long has this been going on?"

He said, "Since he was a child. It has often thrown him into a fire or into water trying to kill him. If you can do anything, help us! Show us compassion!"

Jesus said to him, "'If you can do anything'? All things are possible for the one who has faith."

At that the boy's father cried out, "I have faith; help my lack of faith!"

Noticing that the crowd had surged together, Jesus spoke harshly to the unclean spirit, "Mute and deaf spirit, I command you to come out of him and never enter him again." After screaming and shaking the boy horribly, the spirit came out. The boy seemed to be dead; in fact, several people said that he had died. But Jesus took his hand, lifted him up, and he arose.

Step 2—Make two lists. Create one list with the things that make it hard to believe in God; label that list "My Unbelief." Create a second list with the things that make it easy to believe in God, "My Belief."

Step 3—Pray about it. Going through your "My Unbelief" list one at a time, say:

"God, I believe. Help me understand (insert my unbelief)."

Sit quietly for a few moments and then move on to your next unbelief. Offer the statements to God and see what happens.

Step 4—Create a word cloud or sketch images of any of the answers you get from God. Let these questions guide you:

• What words or phrases are running through your mind?

• What images do you see in your imagination?

• What emotions are you feeling and how can you put them on paper?

Prayer: Holy Spirit, help me understand this journey. Amen.

Stop 2: Examen Prayer

Prayer: Holy Spirit, teach me to have hope along this journey. Amen.

Step 1—Read 2 Peter 3:8-13.

Don't let it escape your notice, dear friends, that with the Lord a single day is like a thousand years and a thousand years are like a single day. The Lord isn't slow to keep his promise, as some think of slowness, but he is patient toward you, not wanting anyone to perish but all to change their hearts and lives. But the day of the Lord will come like a thief. On that day the heavens will pass away with a dreadful noise, the elements will be consumed by fire, and the earth and all the works done on it will be exposed.

Since everything will be destroyed in this way, what sort of people ought you to be? You must live holy and godly lives, waiting for and hastening the coming day of God. Because of that day, the heavens will be destroyed by fire and the elements will melt away in the flames. But according to his promise we are waiting for a new heaven and a new earth, where righteousness is at home.

Step 2—The Examen prayer is a way to pray that uses your imagination, makes you reflect, and connects you in a personal way to God. The prayer can help you to develop a deeper relationship with God, who loves you and wants the best for you. This style of prayer makes you focus on your feelings throughout the day. Feelings like joy, sorrow, peace, and distress are important signs that help you follow God's direction and know God's grace.

Step 3—"Examen" your day following these steps:

A) Remember God is with you:
"[God] is patient toward you, not wanting anyone to perish but all to change their hearts and lives" (2 Peter 3:9).
Think back over your day, and try to see when, where, and how God was with you.
Finish this statement with as many instances of your interaction with God today as you can remember.

God, I know you were with me when . . .

B) Remember your day with gratitude:
"With the Lord a single day is like a thousand years and a thousand years are like a single day" (2 Peter 3:8).
Think back over your day, and focus on the joys and gifts you received. Pay attention to the small things that brought you happiness: what you ate, what you saw, who you spent time with, who cared for you.
Finish this statement with all the things you are thankful for today.

God, thank you for . . .

C) Feel the feels:
"Since everything will be destroyed in this way, what sort of people ought you to be?" (2 Peter 3:11).
Think back over your day, and focus on all the emotions you went through. Pay attention not to the situation that brought the emotion, but ask God to help you understand why you felt that way.
Write down the freshest feelings from today and why you think you felt them.

God, today I felt _____ because _____.

D) Make it right:

"You must live holy and godly lives" (2 Peter 3:11).

Ask God to draw your attention to something that God thinks is particularly important to your life together. Pay attention to the conversation or activity that keeps coming up as you have reviewed your day. Talk with God about that situation.

Write down what you have to say to God or what you need to ask God about the circumstance.

God, so this happened today, and we need to talk about it . . .

E) Move on to tomorrow:

"But according to his promise we are waiting for a new heaven and a new earth, where righteousness is at home" (2 Peter 3:13).

Ask God to be with you in everything that's coming in the next day. Pay attention to any feelings that surface when you think of what tomorrow is to bring.

Write down what you are feeling and surrender those feelings to God.

God, tomorrow is going to bring . . .

Prayer: Holy Spirit, fill me with hope along this journey. Amen.

TRAVELING TOGETHER

CONNECT

Say It with Confidence

Discussion Questions

- What does it feel like for someone to be skeptical of something you believe?

- What does it feel like to have to say something confidently that you aren't sure you fully believe?

- What can you do to gain confidence in saying what you believe?

Broken Telephone

Discussion Questions

- Who had to follow their instruction card? How did it feel to know you had to intentionally change what someone said to you?

- How did you feel when someone intentionally changed the statement you told them? How did you know they did it intentionally?

- Have you ever been in a situation where you had to change how you were going to say something because of the person you were saying it to?

EXPLORE

As you read your assigned passage in your Bible, look for three things:

1. How were people expected to behave?
2. What happens to those who meet the expectations?
3. What happens to those who do not meet expectations?

Group 1: Matthew 25:14-30

- How were people expected to behave?

- What happens to those who meet the expectations?

- What happens to those who do not meet the expectations?

Group 2: Matthew 25:31-46

- How were people expected to behave?

- What happens to those who meet the expectations?

- What happens to those who do not meet the expectations?

REFLECT

"I assure you that when you haven't done it for one of the least of these, you haven't done it for me" (Matthew 25:45).

- Think about a chance you had to tell someone about your faith. Why didn't you do it?

- What prevented you from talking about God's love?

- Write how you wish the conversation had gone instead.

Reason they don't believe:

- A Scripture passage that offers a different point of view/ interpretation to their disbelief:

- An experience in your life that offers an illustration of the "solution" to the problem:

- A reasonable question you could ask the nonbeliever to push them to think more critically about the problem:

Discussion Questions

- How can you use someone's doubt or disbelief to begin a conversation about where God is working in their life?

- Why is it easier to talk about your faith with someone you know is a Christian?

- How do you think a nonbeliever would respond if you started a conversation like this, "I don't know exactly the best way to talk about my faith with you, but I was wondering . . ."

- What is *your* goal for sharing *your* beliefs with others? What do you think God's goal is for you sharing your beliefs with others?

NEXT

Write down one of the problems from the board below. Take fifteen minutes this week and look at a few different denominational websites to see if there is any indication of how the different traditions address the issue. Most of these denominational websites have a "What We Believe" tab or section that will help direct you to some answers.

• What issues do you want to look further into?

• Note a few different ways denominations handle this issue:

• Which way of handling it makes the most sense to you?

Suggested denominational websites:

www.umc.org (The United Methodist Church)

www.ame-church.com (African Methodist Episcopal Church)

www.elca.org (Evangelical Lutheran Church in America)

www.sbc.net (Southern Baptist Convention)

www.abc-usa.org (American Baptist Churches USA)

www.nationalbaptist.com (National Baptist Convention, USA, Inc.)

www.church-of-christ.org/who (Churches of Christ)

www.pcusa.org (Presbyterian Church [USA])

www.episcopalchurch.org (The Episcopal Church)

www.cogic.org (The Church of God in Christ, Inc.)

PRAYER

God, send people into our lives that need to know your love. Help us to come together as your followers to exemplify Christ and bring others to want to know Christ for themselves.

God, help me build a caring relationship with someone who needs your love. Help me become the kind of Christ-like servant that will open the doors to a life with you.

God, bring me opportunities to talk about my relationship with you. Give me the words to talk about the mysteries of Christ, even if I don't fully understand them.

God, fill us with your Holy Spirit to be the light that leads others to you.

In Jesus' name, we pray. Amen.

Lesson 6: Hearing God Speak

SUMMARY

The final leg of this journey is understanding that this is not the end of the road, but more lies ahead in your walk with God. This final push will help you learn how to hear God more clearly.

OVERVIEW

1) **Connect** through thinking about questions or an affirmation activity.

2) **Explore** the call of Rebekah to serve God.

3) **Reflect** on how you would react in Rebekah's situation.

4) **Create** a story portraying different ways to respond to God's call to serve.

5) **Next,** think about the different ways God is calling you to serve now and in the future.

ANCHOR POINT

Genesis 24:57-58—They said, "Summon the young woman, and let's ask her opinion." They called Rebekah and said to her, "Will you go with this man?"

She said, "I will go."

SOLO SEARCHING

Stop 1: Take Up the Mantle

Prayer: God, show me where to go next. Amen.

Step 1—Read Acts 1:15-17, 21-26.

During this time, the family of believers was a company of about one hundred twenty persons. Peter stood among them and said, "Brothers and sisters, the scripture that the Holy Spirit announced beforehand through David had to be fulfilled. This was the scripture concerning Judas, who became a guide for those who arrested Jesus. This happened even though he was one of us and received a share of this ministry" (15-17).

"Therefore, we must select one of those who have accompanied us during the whole time the Lord Jesus lived among us, beginning from the baptism of John until the day when Jesus was taken from us. This person must become along with us a witness to his resurrection." So they nominated two: Joseph called Barsabbas, who was also known as Justus, and Matthias.

They prayed, "Lord, you know everyone's deepest thoughts and desires. Show us clearly which one you have chosen from among these two to take the place of this ministry and apostleship, from which Judas turned away to go to his own place." When they cast lots, the lot fell on Matthias. He was added to the eleven apostles (21-26).

Step 2—Reflect

Why was leadership thrust upon Matthias?

What were the qualifications that allowed Matthias to be chosen as an apostle?

What role did the other apostles play in Matthias's calling?

How can disciples of Jesus still help one another hear God's call?

Step 3—Respond

Read over all your responses from this journey written in your journal. After reading, respond to these questions.

What phrases, words, or themes have come up more than once in your responses?

After reviewing your journey, what is one big thing God is calling you to do?

Prayer: God, show me what to do next. Amen.

Stop 2: Continue

Prayer: God, connect me with people to help me along the journey. Amen.

Step 1—Read 2 Timothy 3:10-17.

But you have paid attention to my teaching, conduct, purpose, faithfulness, patience, love, and endurance. You have seen me experience physical abuse and ordeals in places such as Antioch, Iconium, and Lystra. I put up with all sorts of abuse, and the Lord rescued me from it all! In fact, anyone who wants to live a holy life in Christ Jesus will be harassed. But evil people and swindlers will grow even worse, as they deceive others while being deceived themselves.

But you must continue with the things you have learned and found convincing. You know who taught you. Since childhood you have known the holy scriptures that help you to be wise in a way that leads to salvation through faith that is in Christ Jesus. Every scripture is inspired by God and is useful for teaching, for showing mistakes, for correcting, and for training character, so that the person who belongs to God can be equipped to do everything that is good.

Step 2—Reflect on the Scripture.

Who have you observed live out their faith and calling, like Timothy observed Paul?

How does having a community of believers with you help you to be "proficient and equipped for every good work"?

Step 3—Reflect on your journey: using what you knew before you started this journey and what you have learned along the way, finish the sentences below, creating an affirmation of faith.

Your study leader may ask you to share your affirmation of faith.

I believe God can transform me because . . .

I believe in God because . . .

I believe God made me special because . . .

I believe God loves me because . . .

I believe God loves others because...

I believe God will use me because...

Step 4—Respond

How can you use this affirmation of faith to motivate you on your faith journey after this study ends?

What are some daily practices God is calling you to continue?

Remembering Paul's encouragement of Timothy to keep going, who in your small group will you ask to help you continue working on your relationship with God?

Prayer: God, thank you for transforming my life. Amen.

CONNECT

Twenty-Questions Tag

Discussion Questions

- What was the last question you asked, hoping that the answer would be no?

- When was the last time you freaked out when someone answered your questions with a yes?

- Have you ever said yes to something, knowing it would result in chaos? What made you say yes?

Affirming Each Other

Discussion Questions

- Where there any comments on your poster that surprised you? What were they? Why was it surprising?

- Which was more comfortable for you, writing affirmations or reading your affirmations? Why?

- What do you hear God saying to you through the comments on your poster?

Underline anything said or done that might have made
Rebekah scared, nervous, or unsure.

Circle anything said or done that might have given Rebekah
strength and courage.

*Genesis 24:50-61: Laban and Bethuel both responded, "This is all the
Lord's doing. We have nothing to say about it. Here is Rebekah, right
in front of you. Take her and go. She will be the wife of your master's
son, just as the Lord said." When Abraham's servant heard what they
said, he bowed low before the Lord. The servant brought out gold
and silver jewelry and clothing and gave them to Rebekah. To her
brother and to her mother he gave the finest gifts. He and the men
with him ate and drank and spent the night.*

*When they got up in the morning, the servant said, "See me off to my
master." Her brother and mother said, "Let the young woman stay
with us not more than ten days, and after that she may go." But he
said to them, "Don't delay me. The Lord has made my trip successful.
See me off so that I can go to my master." They said, "Summon the
young woman, and let's ask her opinion." They called Rebekah and
said to her, "Will you go with this man?"*

She said, "I will go."

*So they sent off their sister Rebekah, her nurse, Abraham's servant,
and his men. And they blessed Rebekah, saying to her,*

*"May you, our sister, become
    thousands of ten thousand;
may your children possess
        their enemies' cities."*

*Rebekah and her young women got up, mounted the camels, and
followed the man. So the servant took Rebekah and left.*

Discussion Questions

- Of all the scary situations that we named, which one do you think would have required the most trust from Rebekah? Why?

- How do you think people learn to trust God?

- Are there any of these instances that provided strength or courage for any of the specific fears we named earlier?

- How can we recognize God calming our fears?

REFLECT

Genesis 24:57-58: They said, "Summon the young woman, and let's ask her opinion." They called Rebekah and said to her, "Will you go with this man?"

She said, "I will go."

- Imagine what it would have been like to be Rebekah.

- What kind of things do you think you would be feeling?

- What questions would you want to ask?

- If someone were to tell you that as an answer to a prayer, God was asking you to leave your family, who would you want to talk to before you decided? What would you want to say to them?

CREATE

Create a skit that demonstrates how your group thinks God would go about accomplishing God's goal. Think of how the situation might cause fear or uncertainty, and how God would provide courage and strength. After ten minutes, each group will share their skit or tell their story with everyone.

Group 1 —Prompt: A Christian adult advisor is praying that a certain student will join a school club to provide a positive Christian example for others in the club.

God's Goal: Students sharing their faith.

Group 2 —Prompt: A student in a youth group prays that a certain adult will begin to help lead youth group.

God's Goal: For the student and the adult to use their gifts to grow God's kingdom.

Group 3—Prompt: A refugee student prays for God to provide her family a church to make them feel more welcome in their new community.

God's Goal: For God's children to share love with the hurt and lonely.

NEXT

Joshua 1:5-6: I will be with you in the same way I was with Moses. I won't desert you or leave you. Be brave and strong, because you are the one who will help this people take possession of the land, which I pledged to give to their ancestors.

Write down three ways God is calling you to be in service.

1—In the next month:

2—After you finish school:

3—When you get a job:

PRAYER

Using a Bible, select one of the following blessings to pray aloud over your brothers and sisters in Christ.

Romans 15:5-6

Romans 15:13

2 Corinthians 13:13

Ephesians 6:23-24

1 Thessalonians 3:12-13

2 Peter 3:18